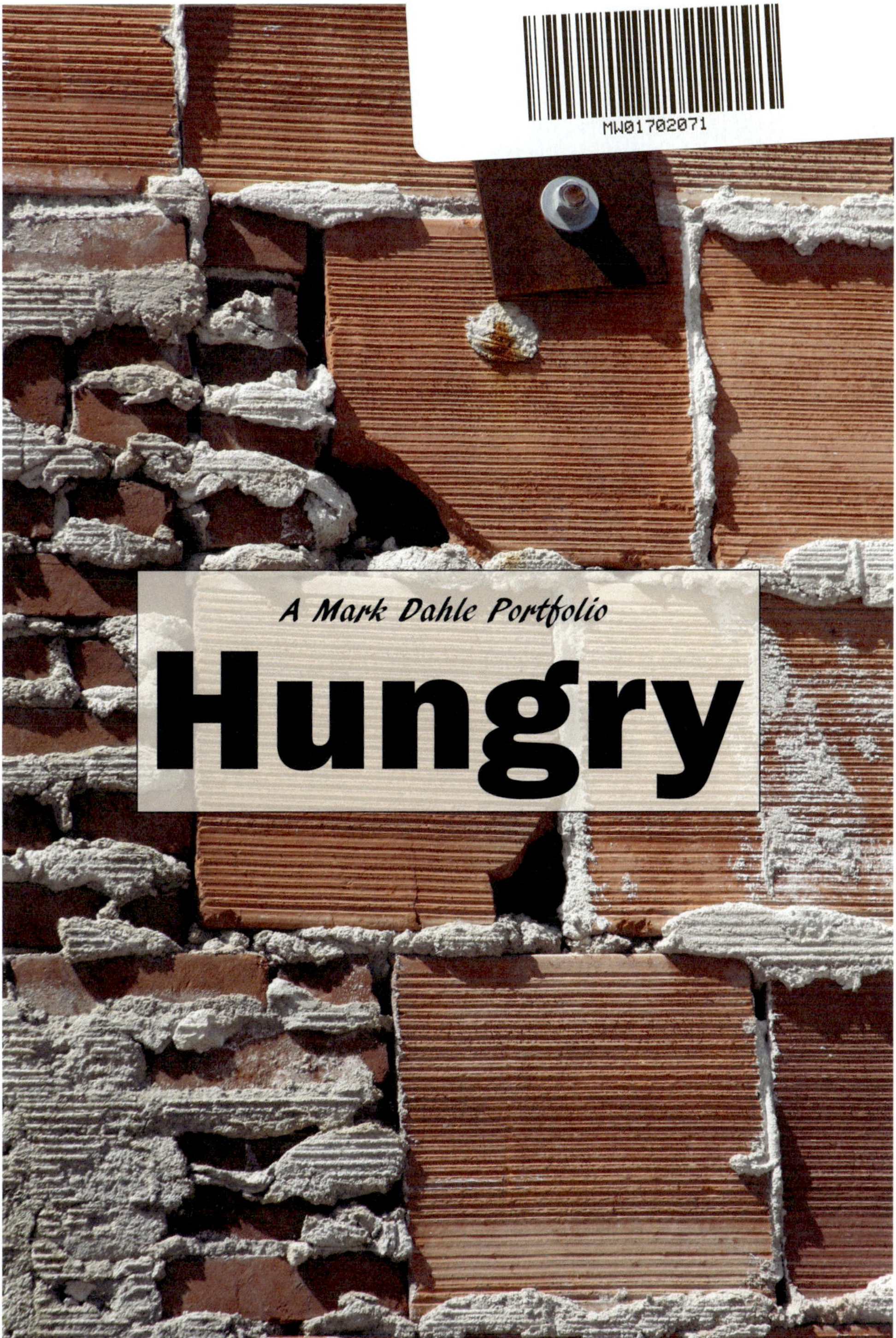

A Mark Dahle Portfolio

Hungry

Mark Dahle Portfolios can be read in a few minutes and enjoyed for a lifetime.

This portfolio includes a story about a hungry girl invited to Thanksgiving Dinner, a photo of a beautiful 36 x 24 inch painting from Mark Dahle's "Stop and Go" series (at the right) and twenty-five outstanding photographs from Amsterdam and San Diego.

Unlike many picture books, the text is unrelated to the paintings and photographs. This might seem weird at first. One thing that helps is to order more portfolios until you get used to it. Feel free to draw your own pictures of Thanksgiving turkeys and side dishes on the pages if you like.

Photographs in this book are available in limited editions. See http://www.MarkDahle.com for more information and for previews of upcoming portfolios.

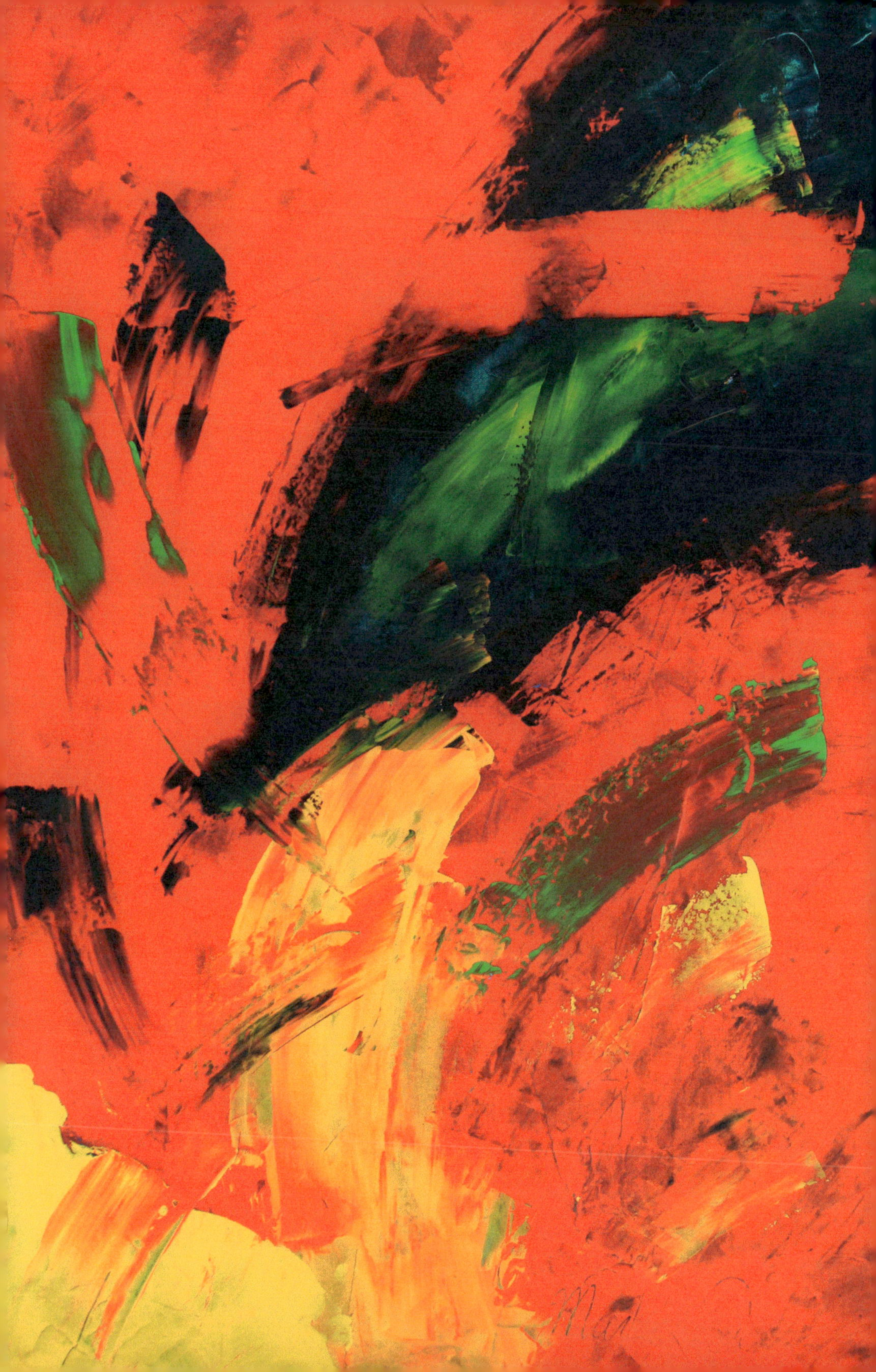

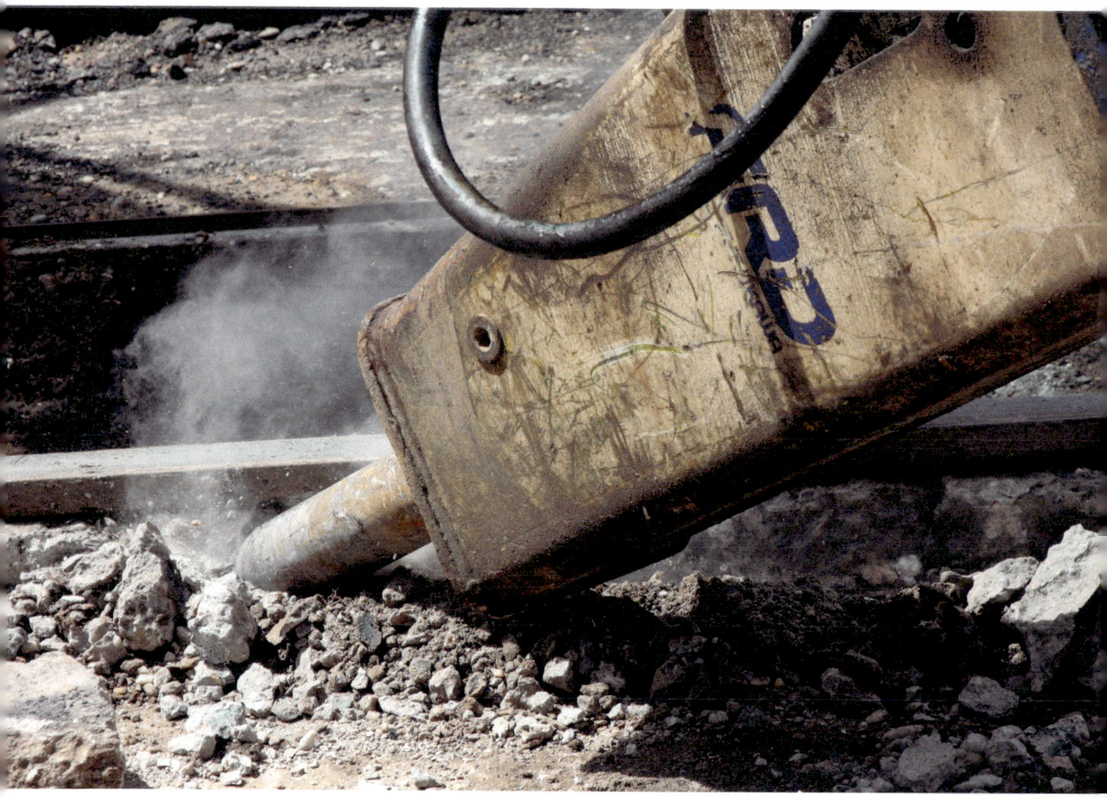

Sally is hungry.
She's been hungry all afternoon.
But she's in luck!
It's Thanksgiving Day.

At this very moment,
downstairs on the dining room table,
all the best china is laid out.

The silver is polished.
The crystal water glasses are filled.
The wine is ready to be poured.
The napkins are in place.
Extra leaves have been added to the table
so it will hold all the food
and all the guests.

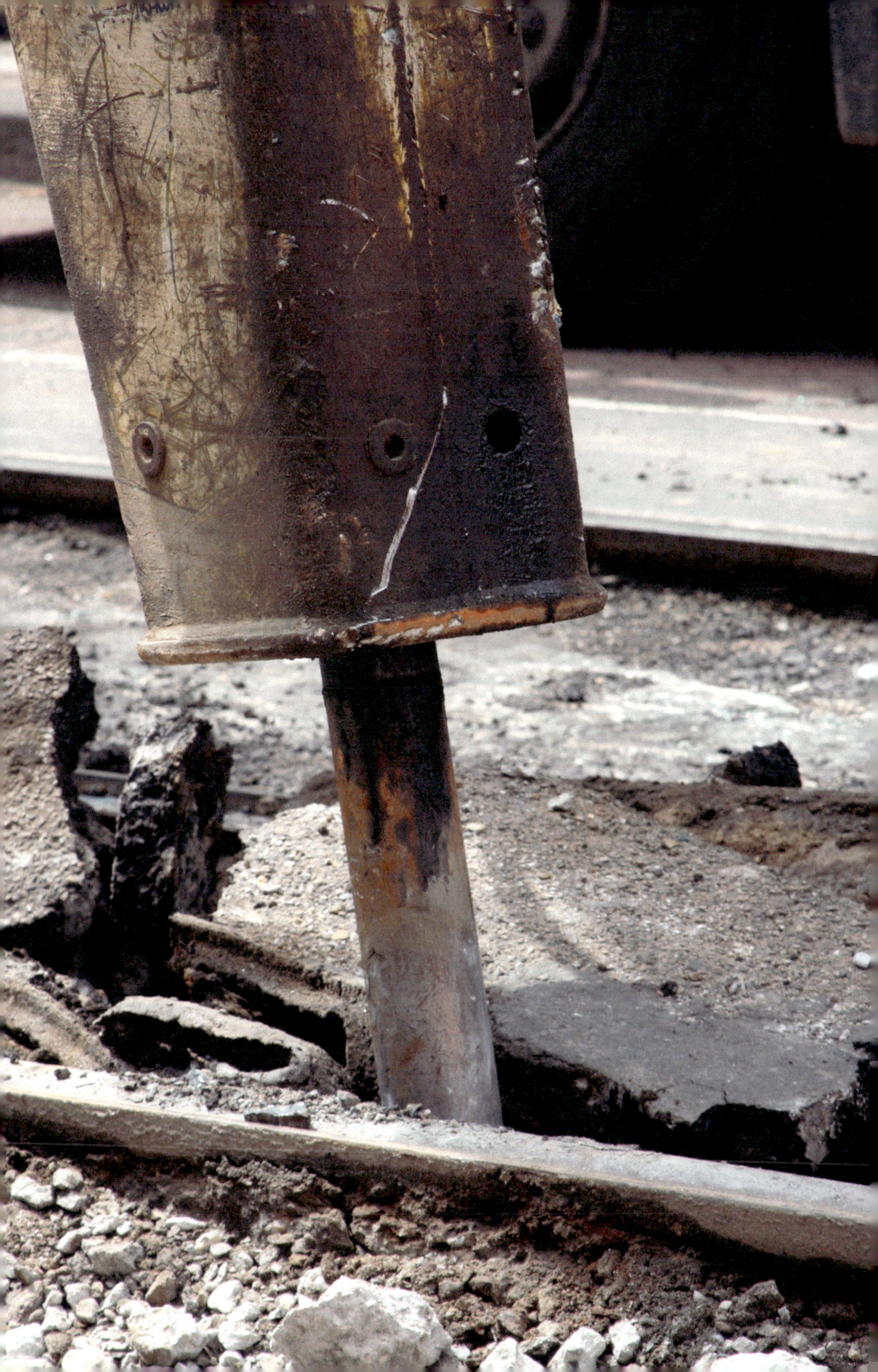

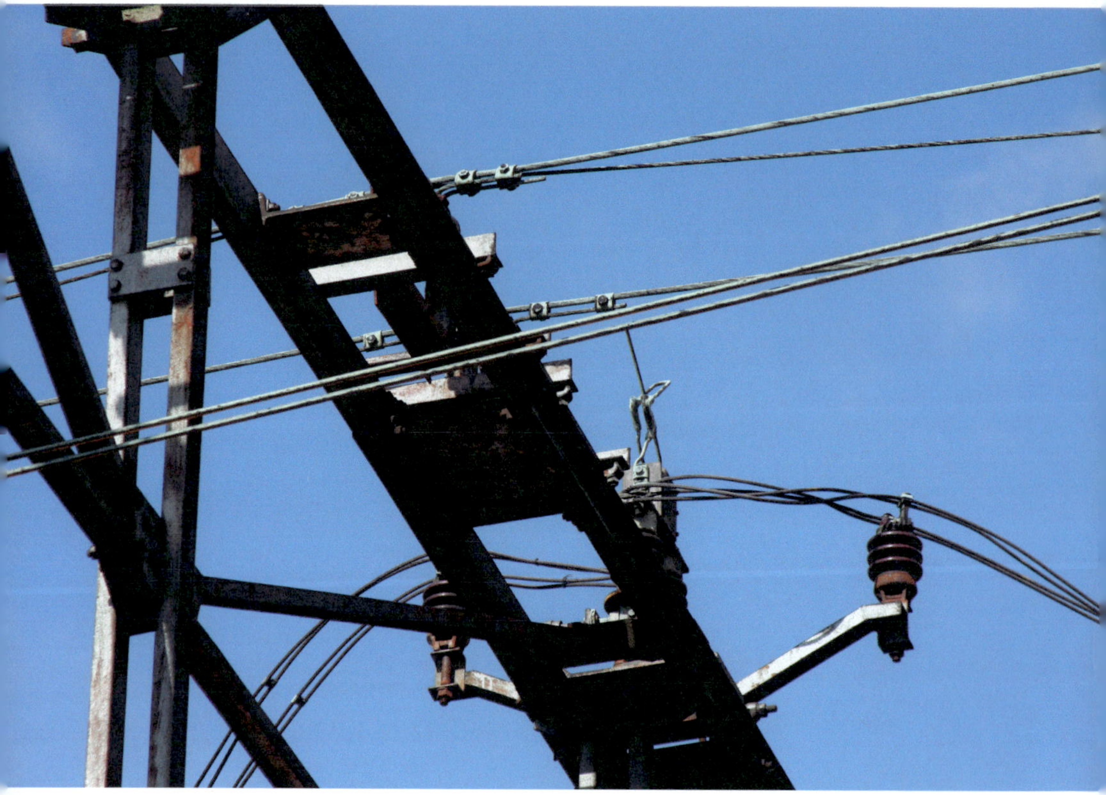

On the table is a turkey,
steaming,
golden to perfection.

Sally’s dad has just finished carving it.

Next to the turkey
is a plate of delicious cranberry jelly.

Sally's mom is slicing the homemade bread,
still warm from the oven.

Real butter and blackberry jam
are already on the table.

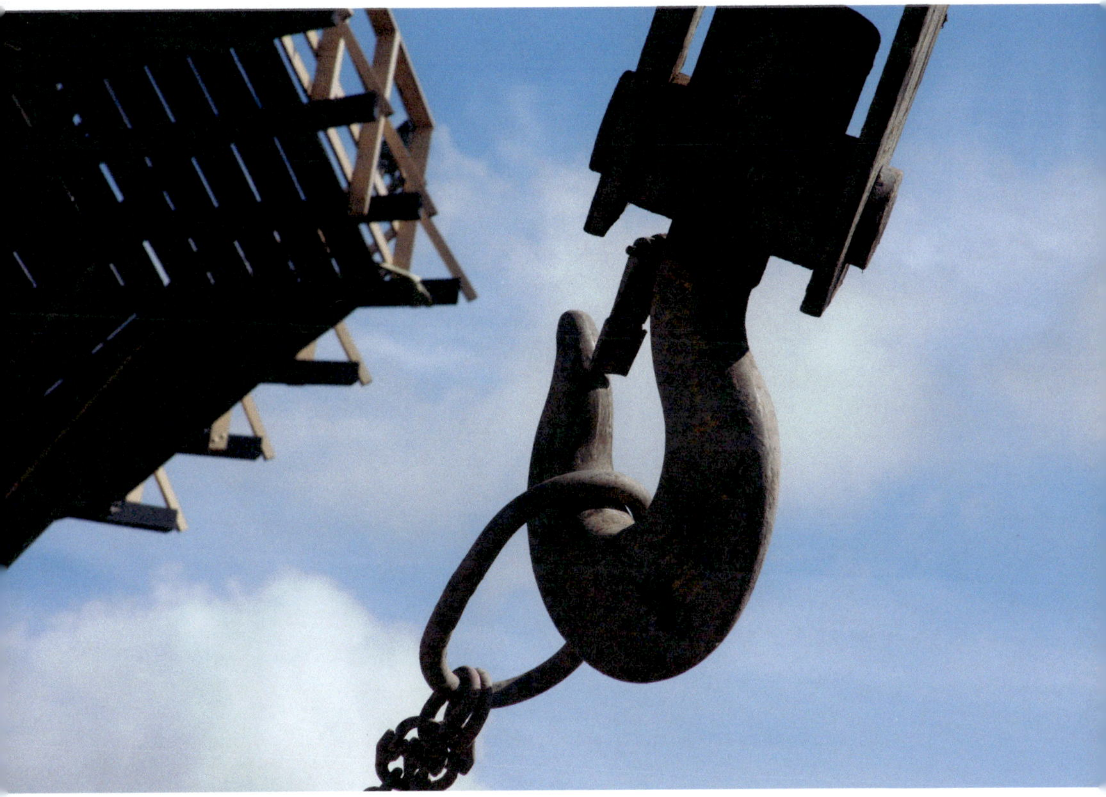

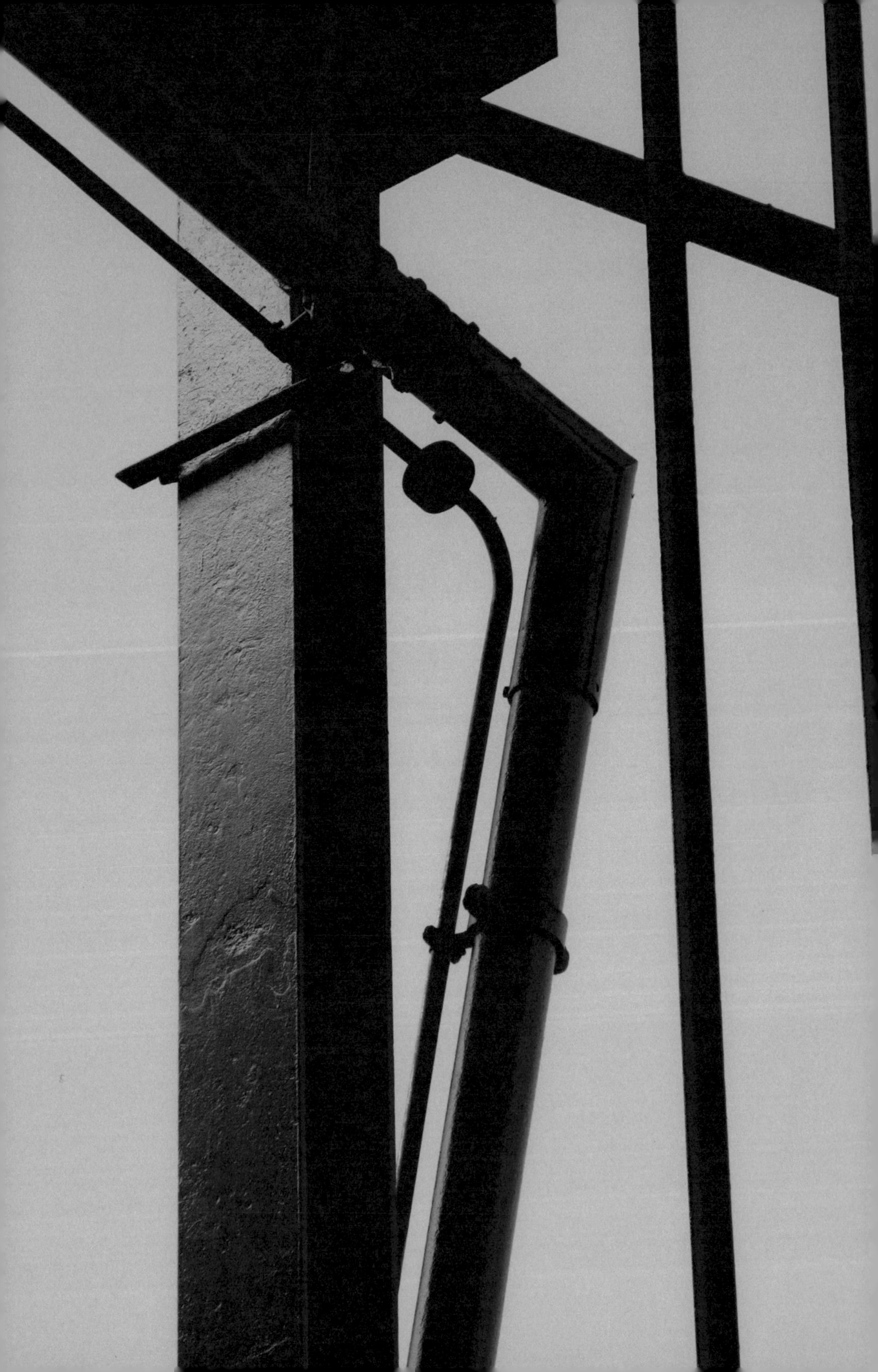

Also on the table are the vegetables.
A steaming bowl of borscht.
String beans cooked in mushroom soup,
with baked onions on top.
Corn boiled in milk.
Candied yams.
Saag with naan.
Aloo Matar.
Steamed carrots.
Steamed broccoli with lemon juice.
An appetizer tray of sliced carrots and celery,
black olives and green olives,
watercress and radishes.

The table holds five salads:
a tossed green salad
with pecans, avocados and cranberries,
a three-bean salad,
a fruit salad with mangos and papaya and kiwi,
a bowl of tabbouleh,
and a German potato salad.

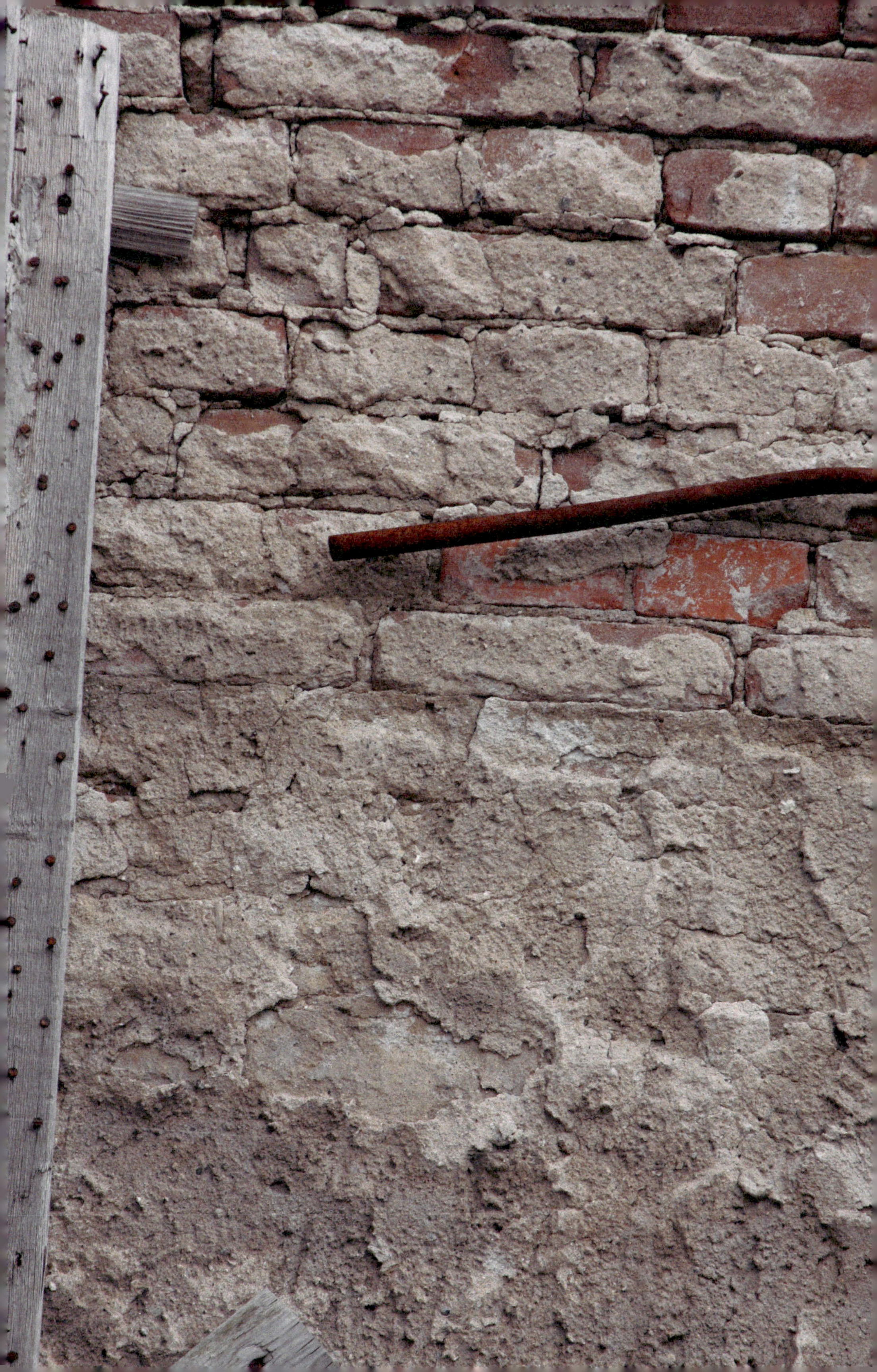

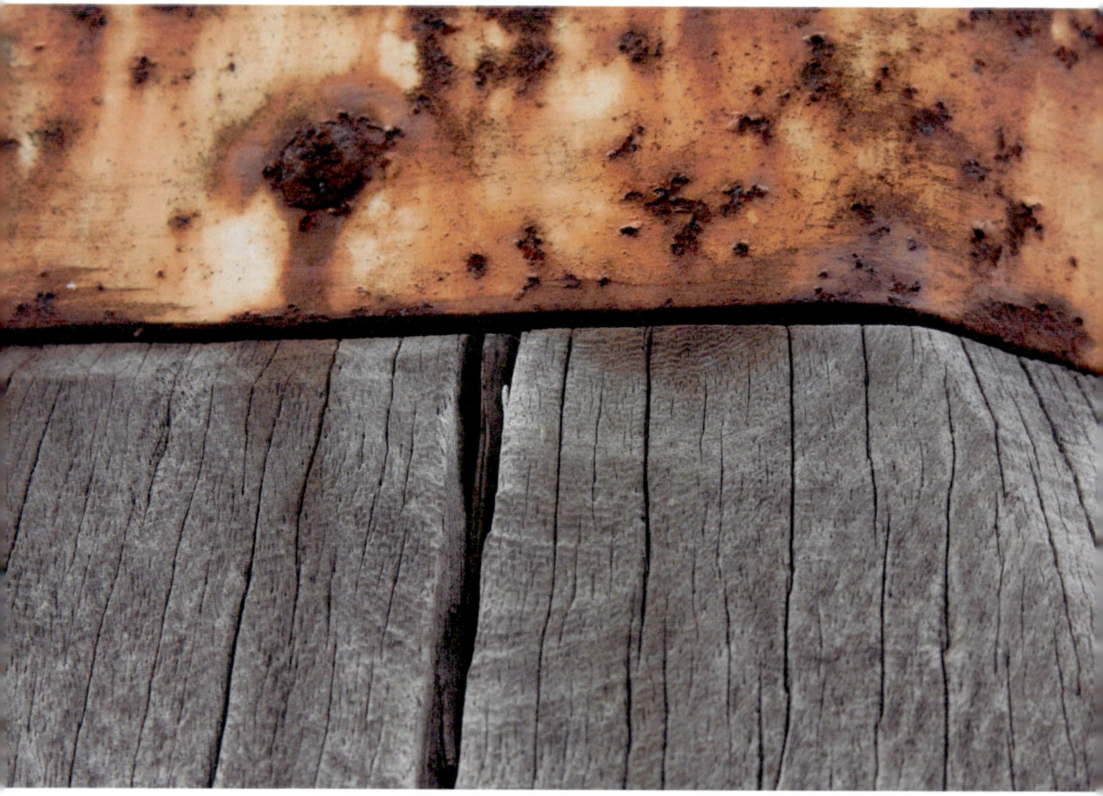

Near the salads:
a huge bowl
of hot mashed potatoes,
with gravy right beside it,
still steaming.

And next to that, four kinds of rice:
brown rice
steamed rice
fried rice
and safron rice.

Near that is the stuffing,
wonderfully moist,
made with apples and nuts
and baked inside the turkey.

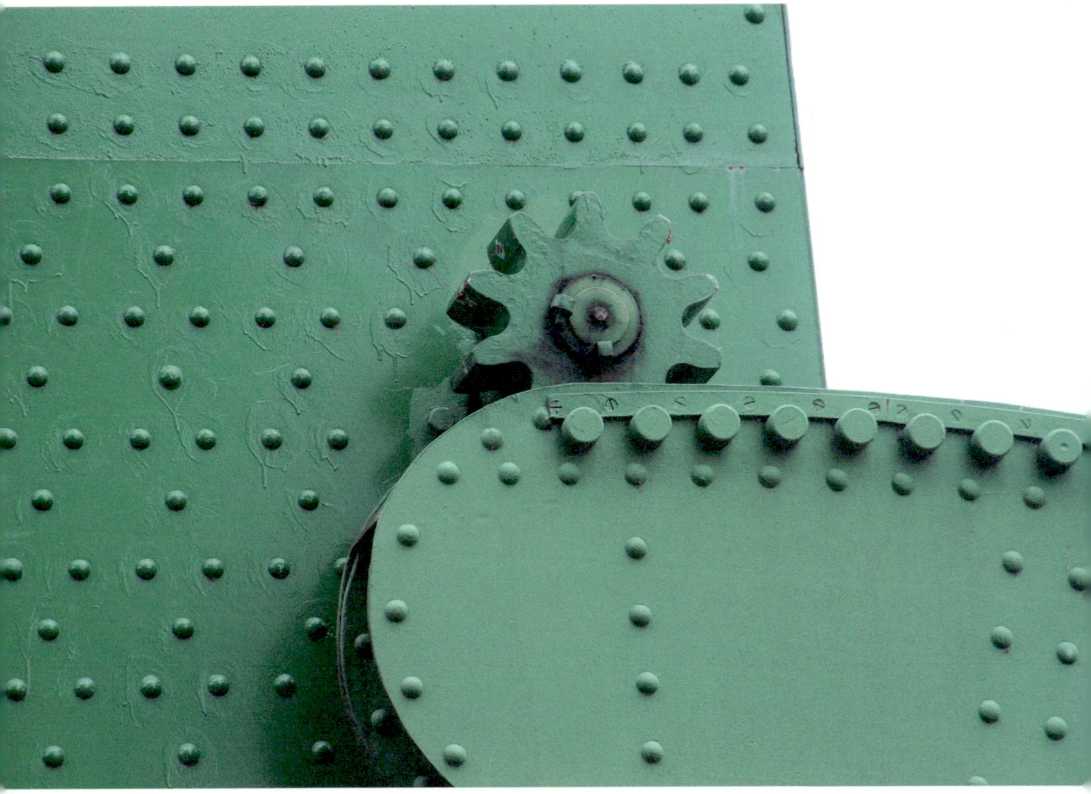

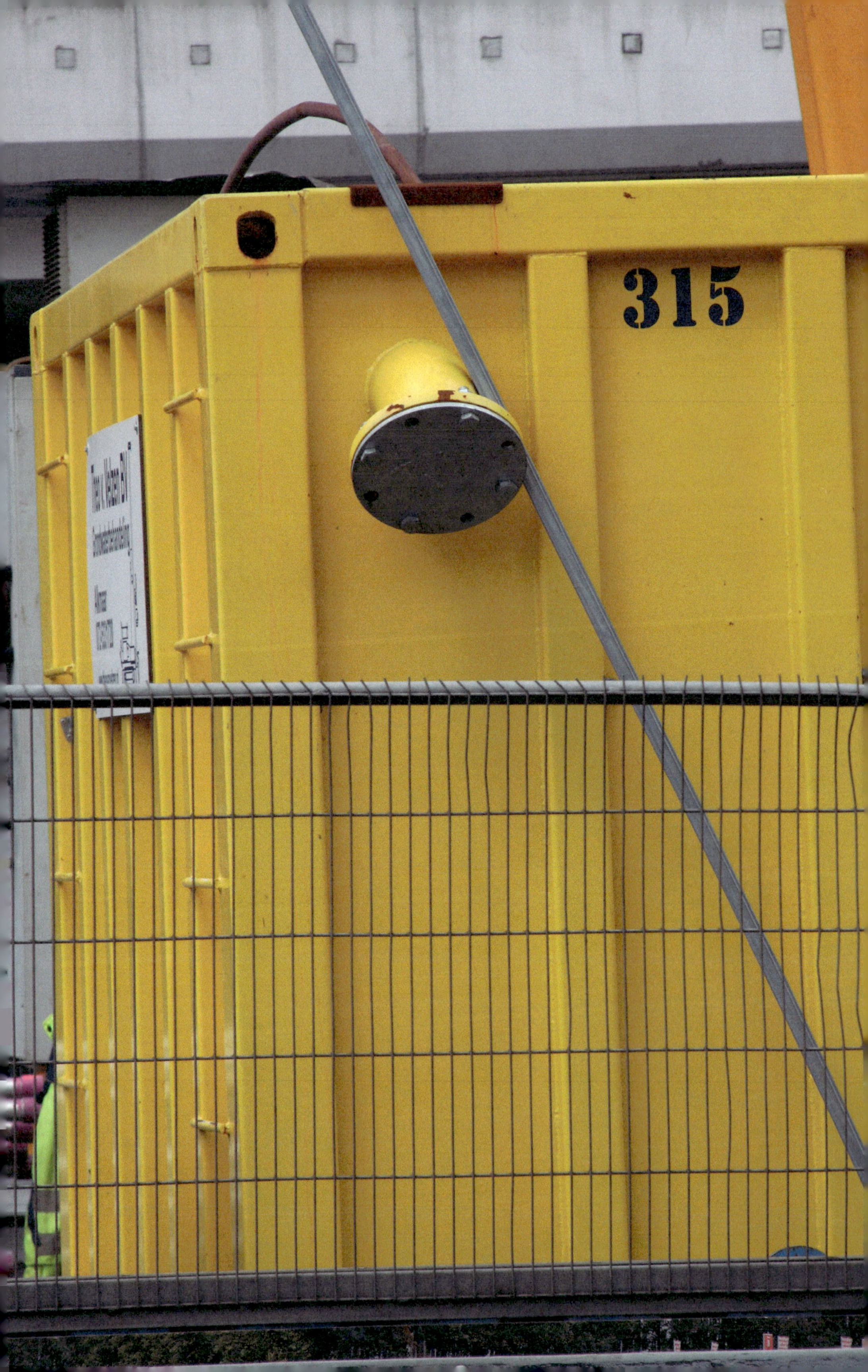
315

Eight dishes on the table
have lids on them --
you can't even see what they are --
but the smells coming from them are wonderful.

You can smell spices from China
and Peru and Thailand
and the Middle East.

The smells have been
floating up the stairs to Sally's room,
where she's very hungry.
She's been hungry all afternoon.

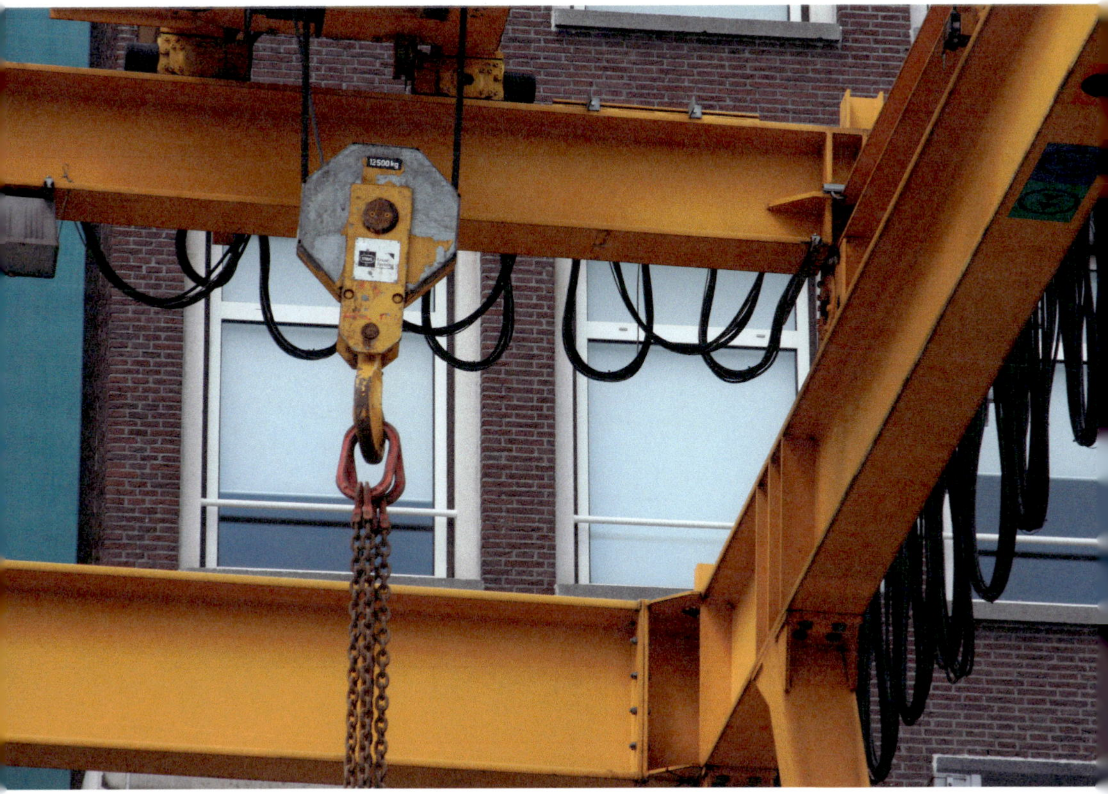
12500 kg

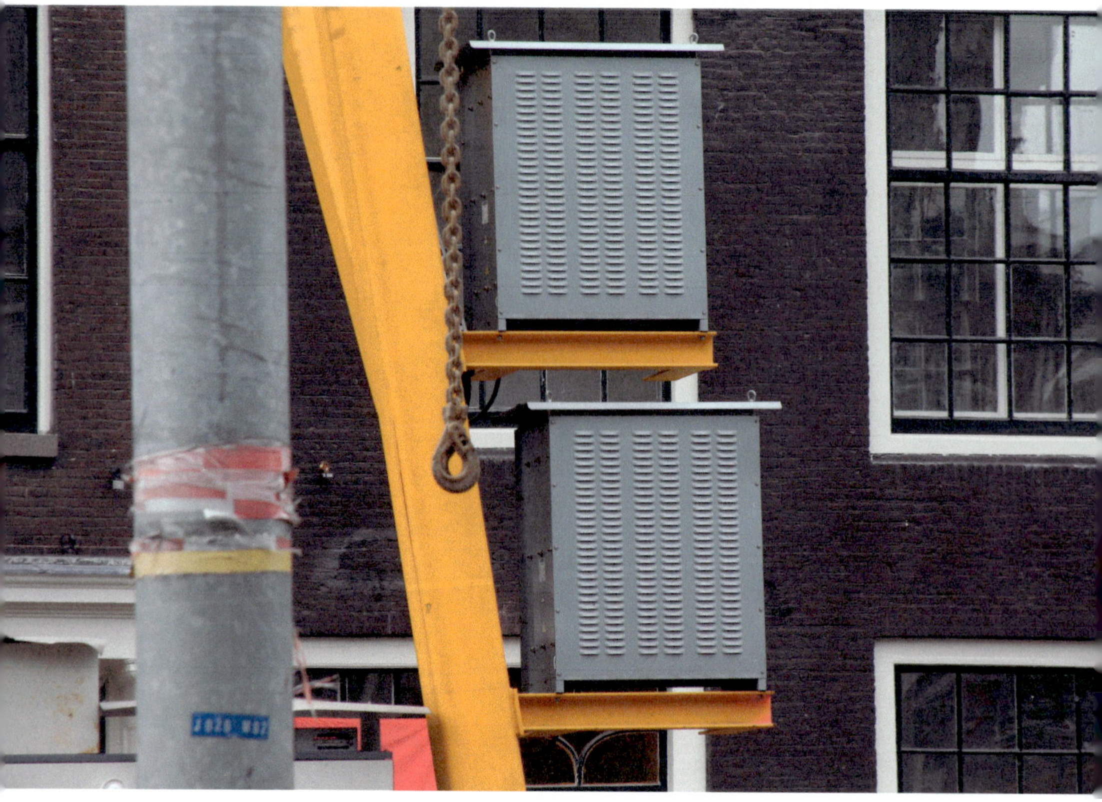

On the table,
there's even some Jell-O --
lime green with cottage cheese
and pineapple chunks
and a separate bowl
of raspberry Jell-O
with real raspberries and sliced bananas.

In the kitchen, there’s a dessert tray:
Apple pie
Blackberry pie
Pumpkin pie
Banana cream pie
Mincemeat pie
And cookies -- ten different kinds of cookies.
In the fridge: real whipping cream.
In the freezer: five kinds of ice cream.

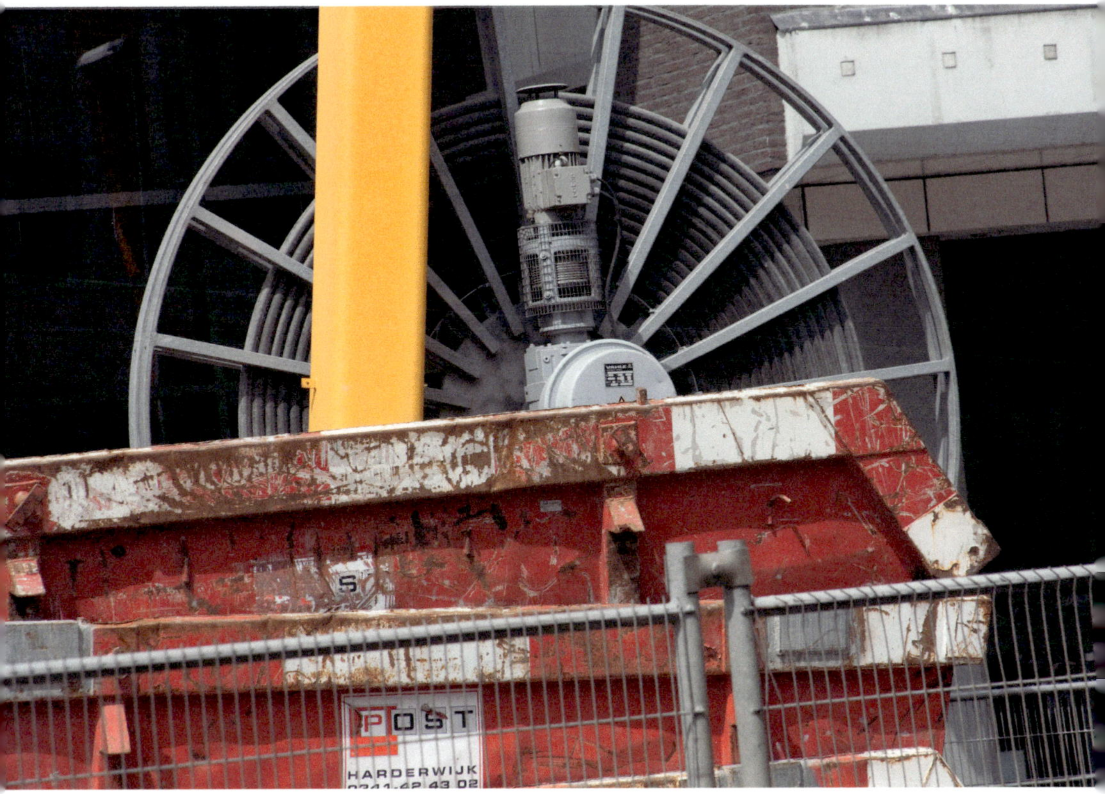
POST
HARDERWIJK

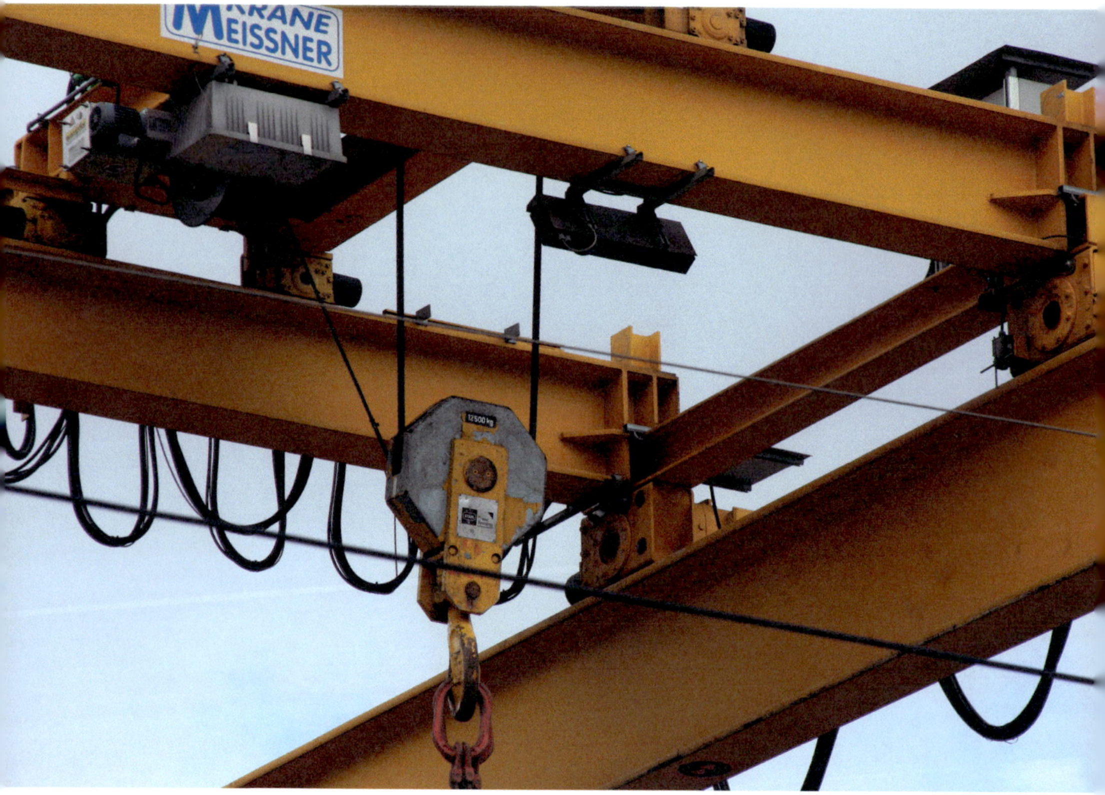
KRANE
MEISSNER
12500 kg

A feast!
And it's ready!
The moment has come.

Sally's mom calls out,
"Sally, come down for dinner!
Everything is ready!"

It's the moment she's been waiting for.

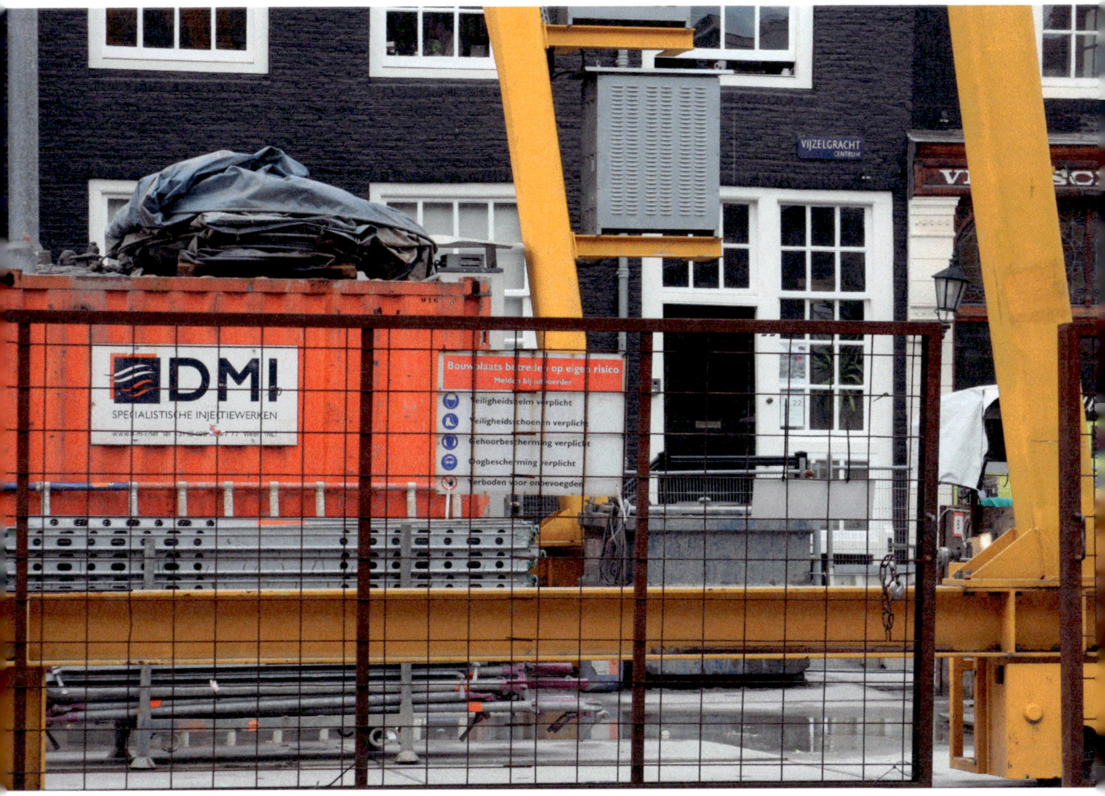
VIJZELGRACHT
CENTRUM
DMI
SPECIALISTISCHE INJECTIEWERKEN
Bouwplaats betreden op eigen risico
Melden bij uitvoerder
Veiligheidshelm verplicht
Veiligheidsschoenen verplicht
Gehoorbescherming verplicht
Oogbescherming verplicht
Verboden voor onbevoegden

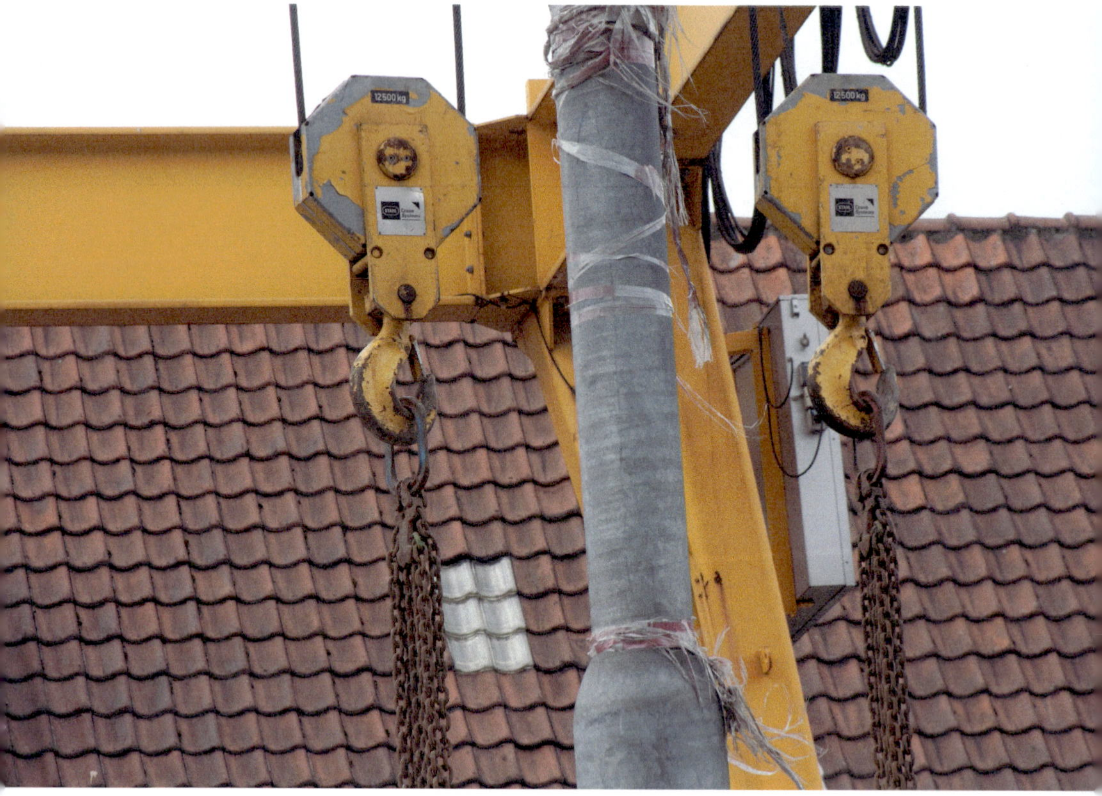
12500 kg
12500 kg

But up in her room,
Sally doesn't believe the call.

For some reason,
even though Sally is hungry,
she doesn't believe the call is for *her*,
at least not right now.

Maybe she’s working on something
that she doesn’t want to leave.
Maybe she thinks the food won’t be that good.
(She hasn’t seen it yet.)
Maybe she’s shy
and doesn’t think she’s good enough
to come eat with everyone.
Maybe she doesn’t like someone
who’s been invited
and she doesn’t want to sit with her.
Maybe . . .
Whatever the reason,
Sally doesn’t believe the call.

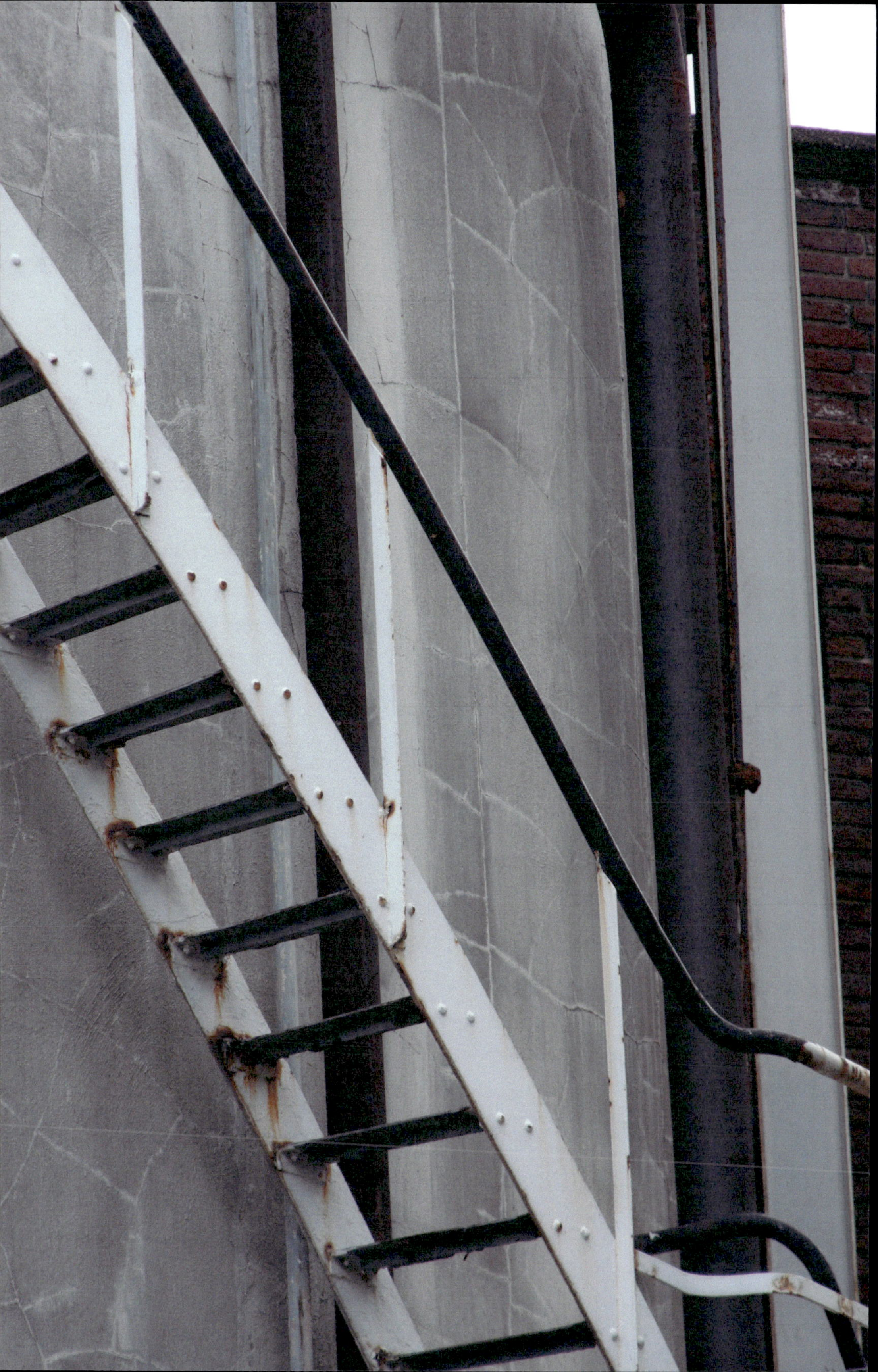

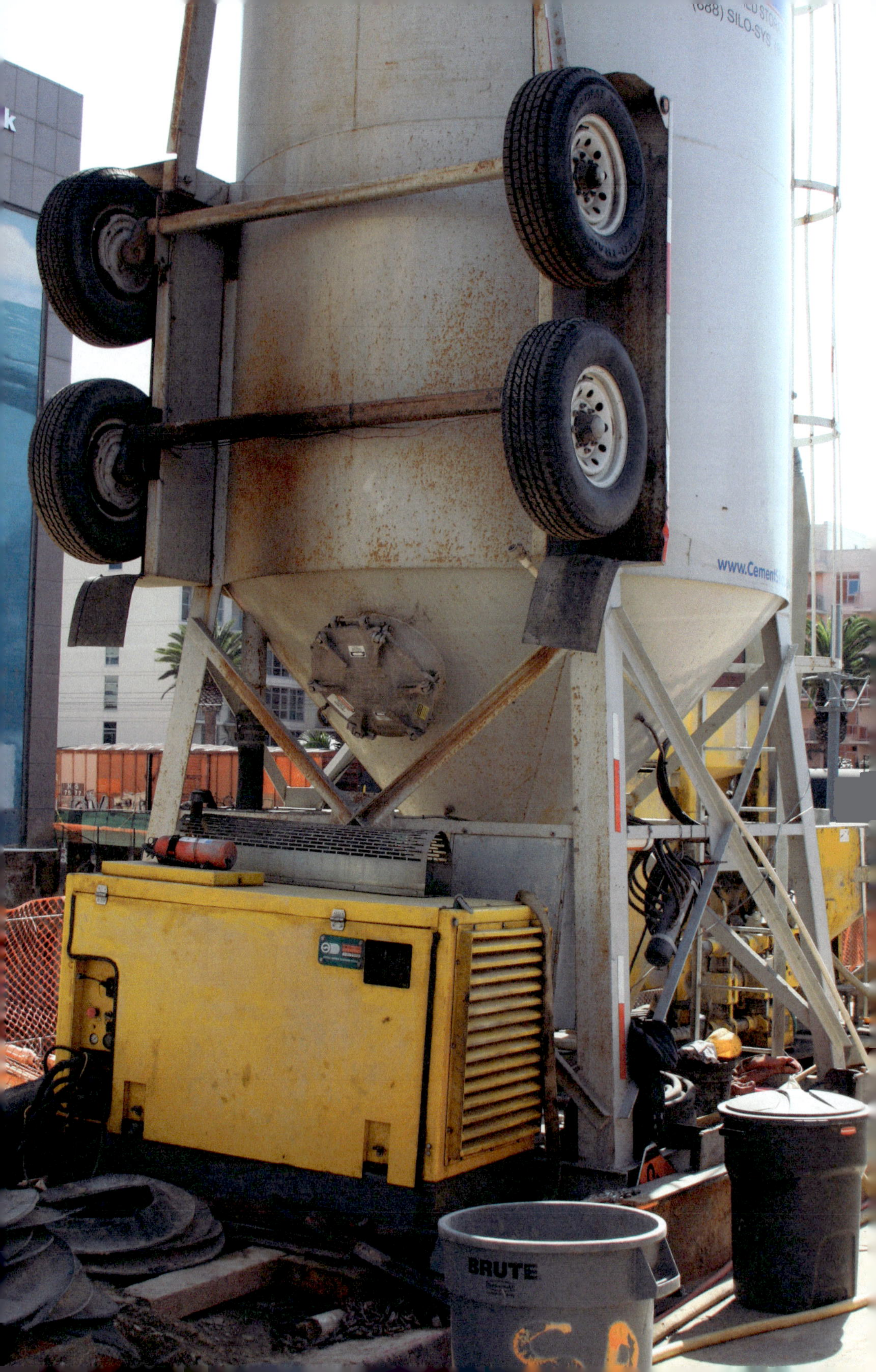
SILO-SYS
BRUTE

"No," she says to herself,
"It's too early.
Mom can't mean that I should come *now*."

Thanksgiving Dinner is ready.
Sally's place is set.
The food is prepared.
The other guests are in place.

If Sally persists,
will her hunger be satisfied?

Downstairs, with all the commotion
of relatives and friends washing their hands
and getting to the table,
it takes a while
before people notice
that Sally is still missing.

"Sally, dinner."
Her mom repeats the call.
This time it's a little more urgent.

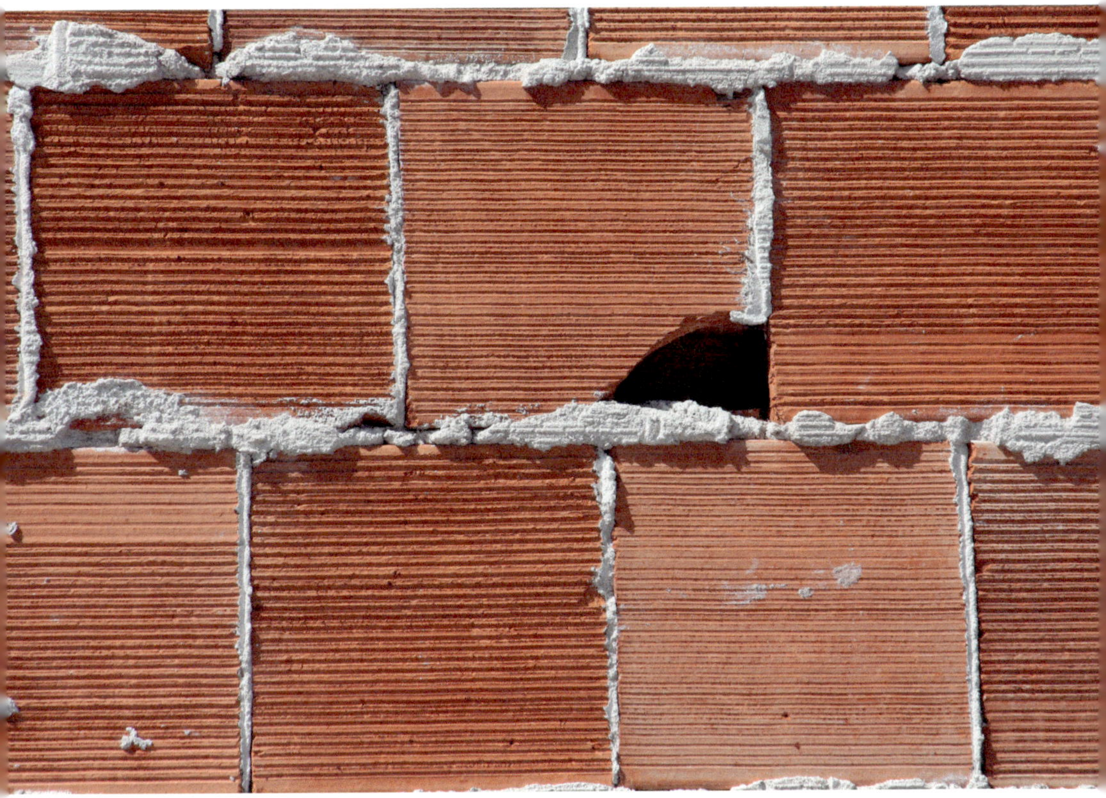

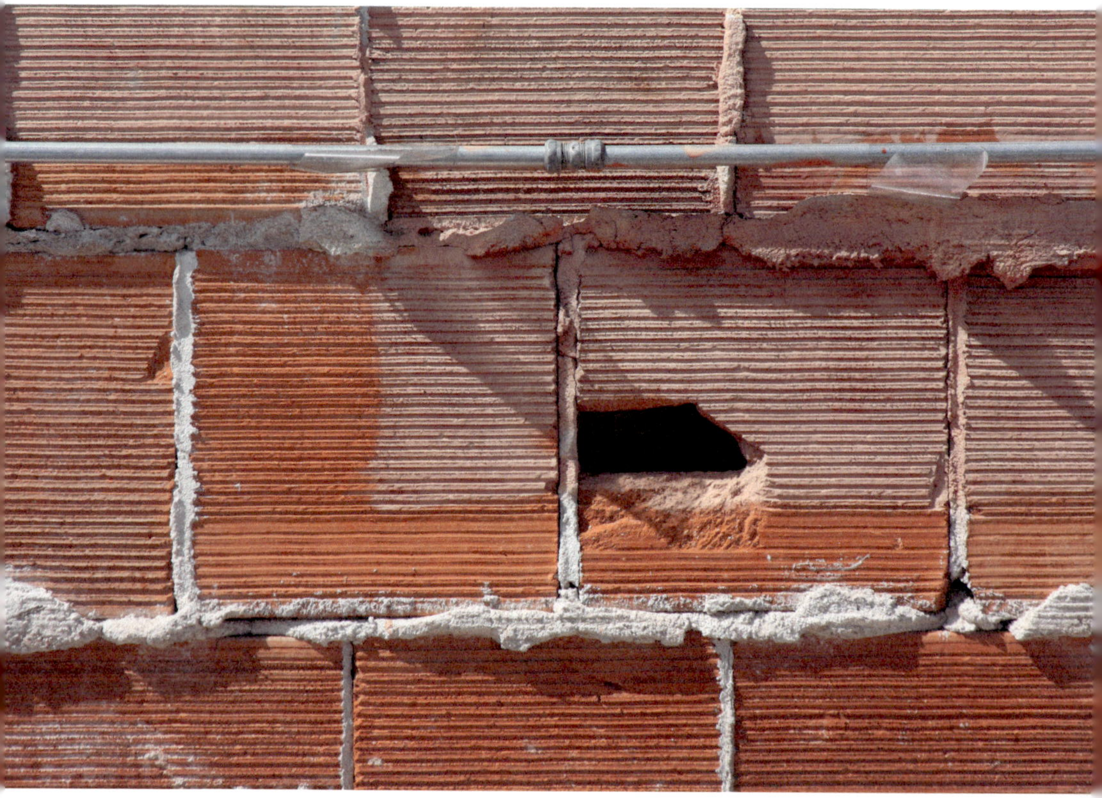

Sally hears the call.
But she still doesn't believe it means her,
right now.

Maybe she's working on something
that she doesn't want to leave.
Maybe she thinks the food won't be that good.
Maybe she's shy
and doesn't think she's good enough
to come eat with everyone.
Maybe she doesn't like someone
who's been invited
and she doesn't want to sit with her.
Maybe . . .

“Sally Jones, mind your mother
and come down here right now!”

That’s her father.

Sally had been busy on something,
and hadn’t been paying much attention before.
But she is startled by her father’s urgency.
Now she believes the call.
It’s for her.
This is the time.

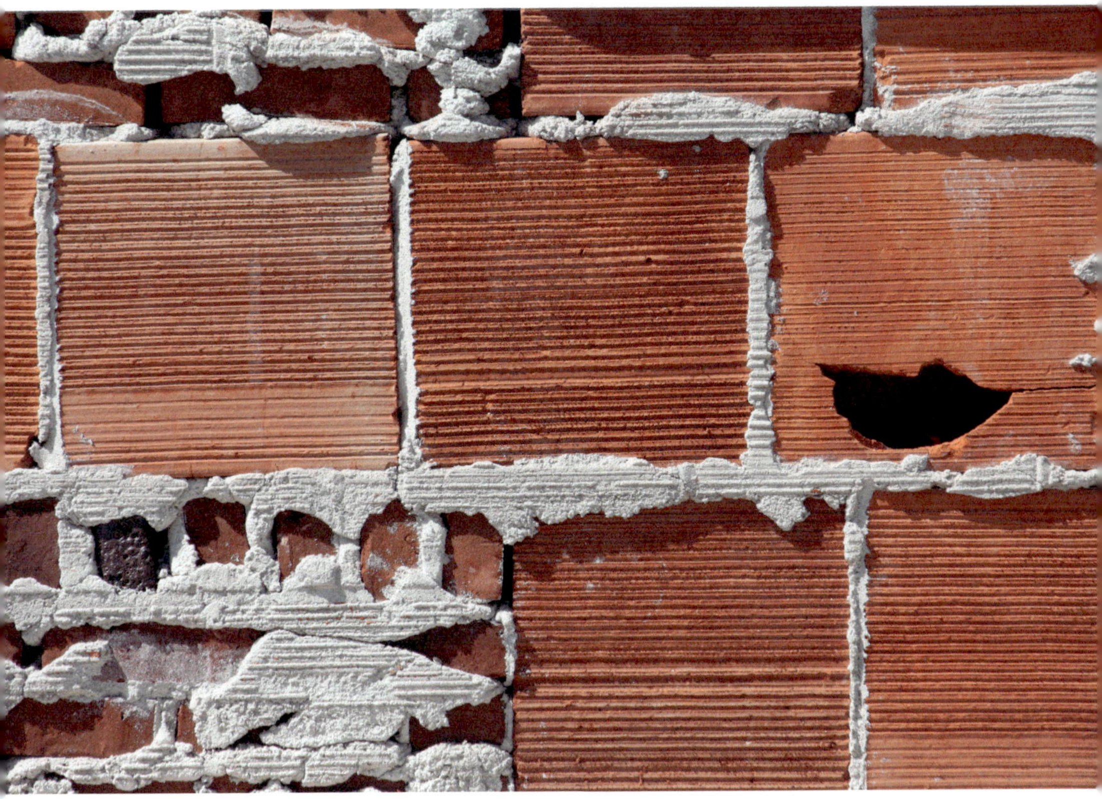

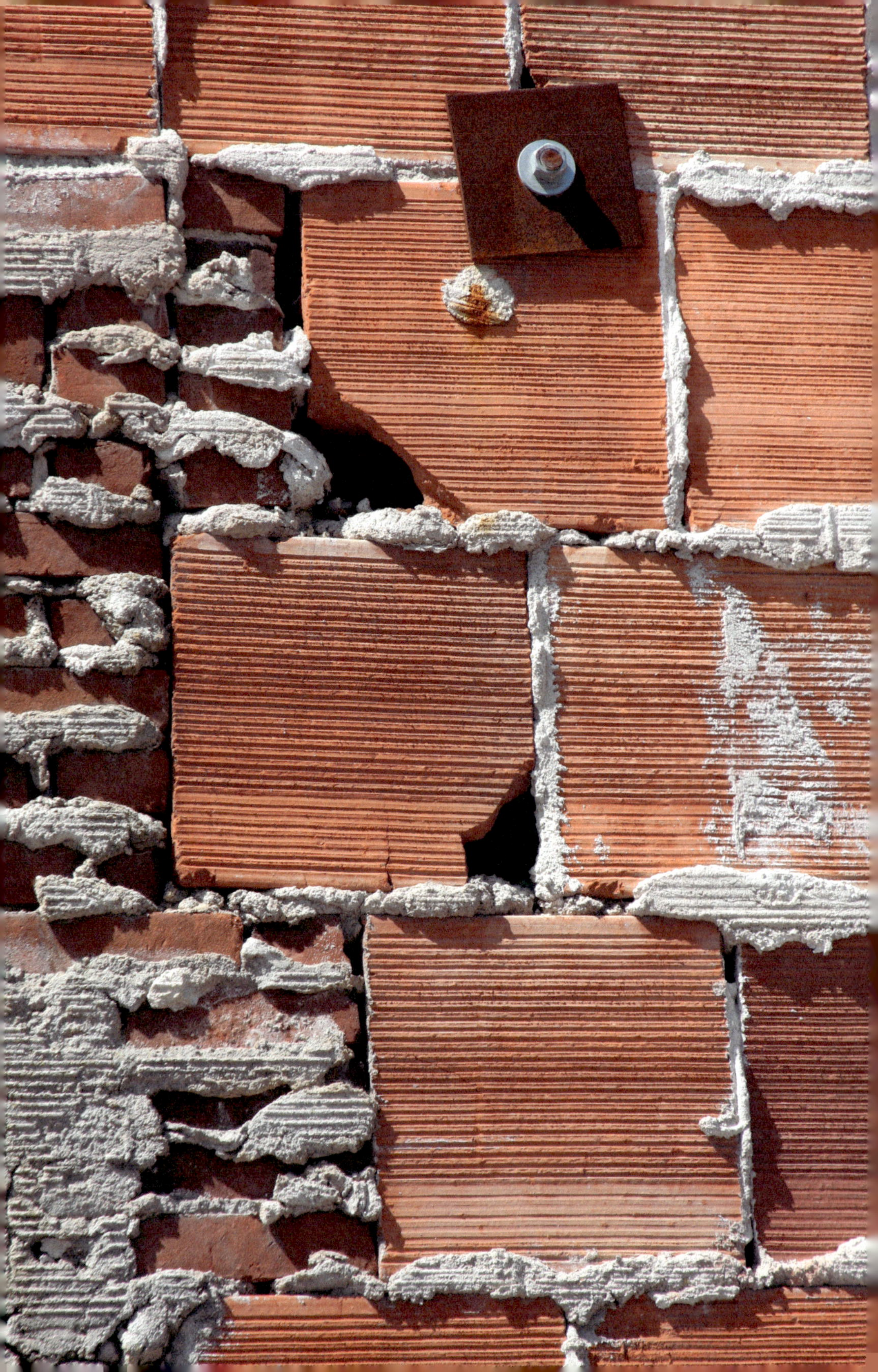

Sally realizes all the guests will be looking at her when she arrives late.

She doesn't want to face that.
Not just yet.

The guests might not have a good opinion of her if she just caves in all at once.

So now she believes the call,
but doesn't act.

As long as she persists in this stance --
as long as she believes the call but doesn't act --
will her hunger be satisfied?

Is she any better off than before?

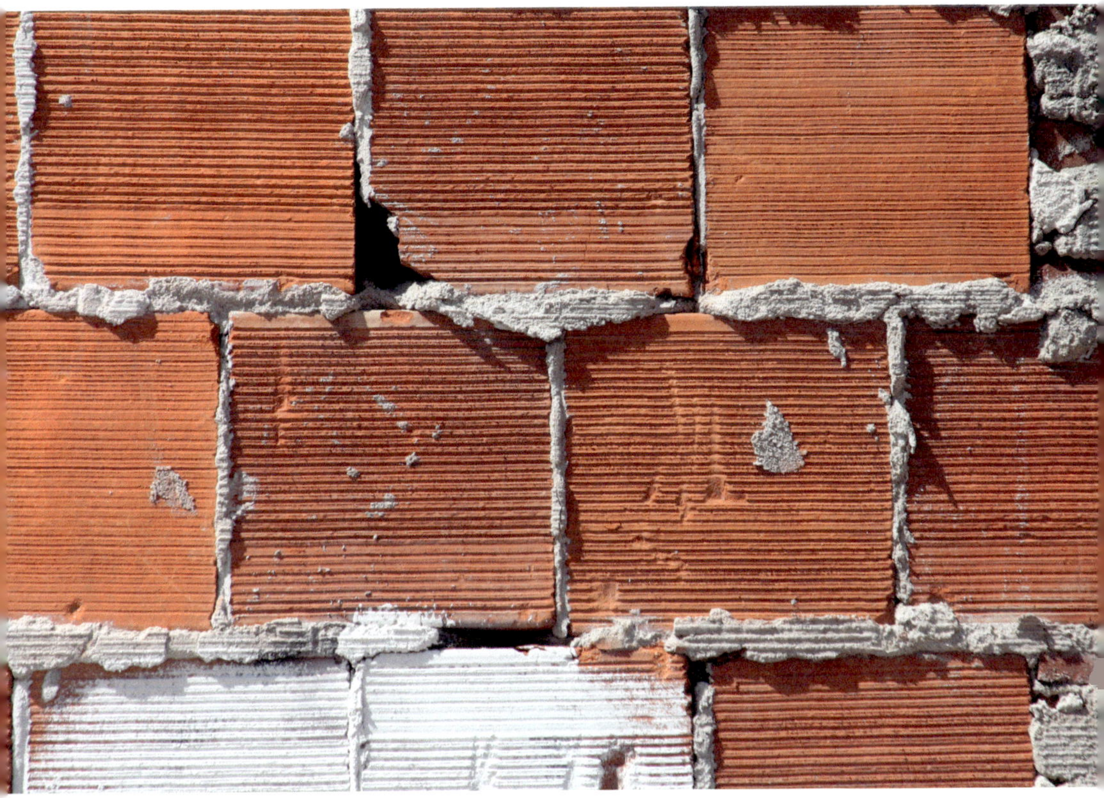

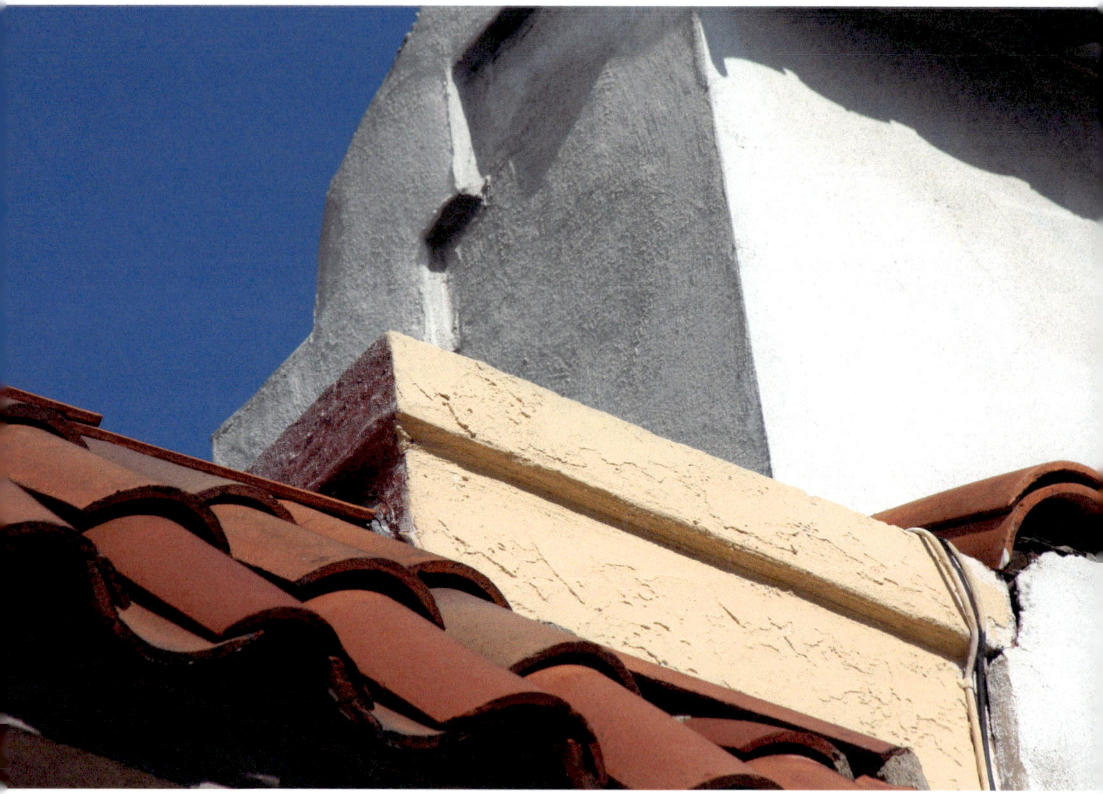

Even if Sally refuses to learn, maybe you can.

What wonderful meals are *you* missing
just because you don't think they're for you?

It's time to pull up a chair at the table and rejoice!

It's Thanksgiving Day!

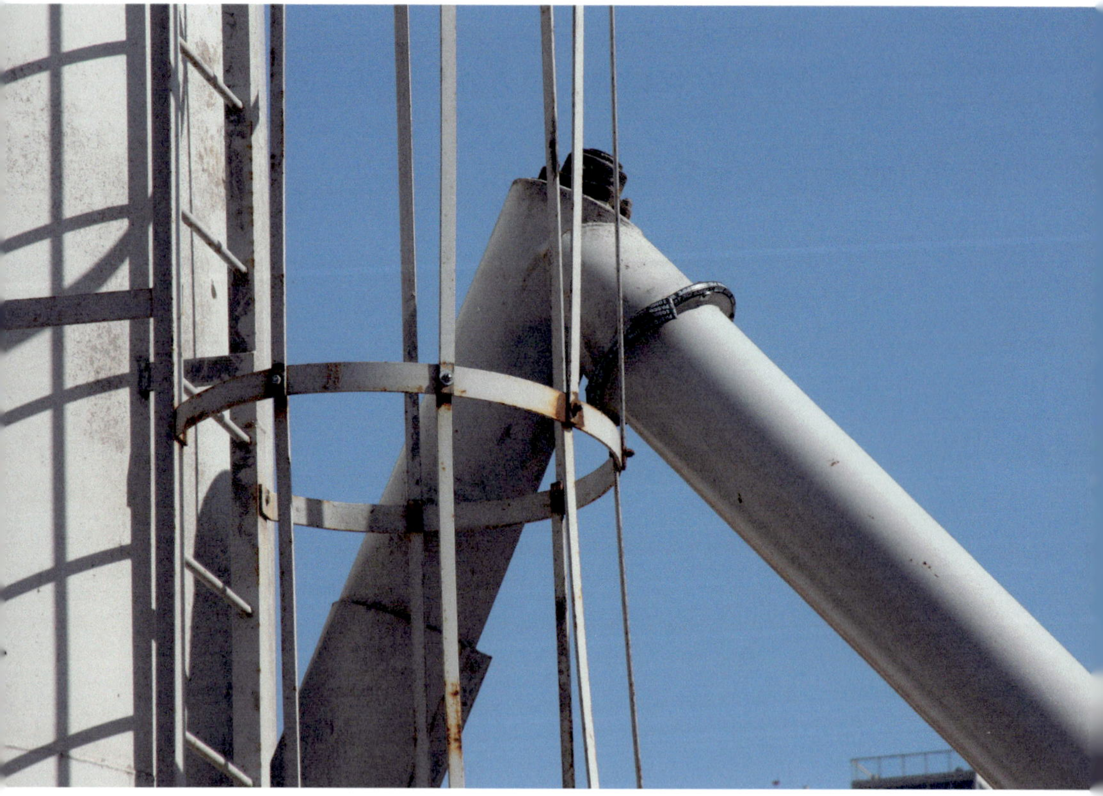

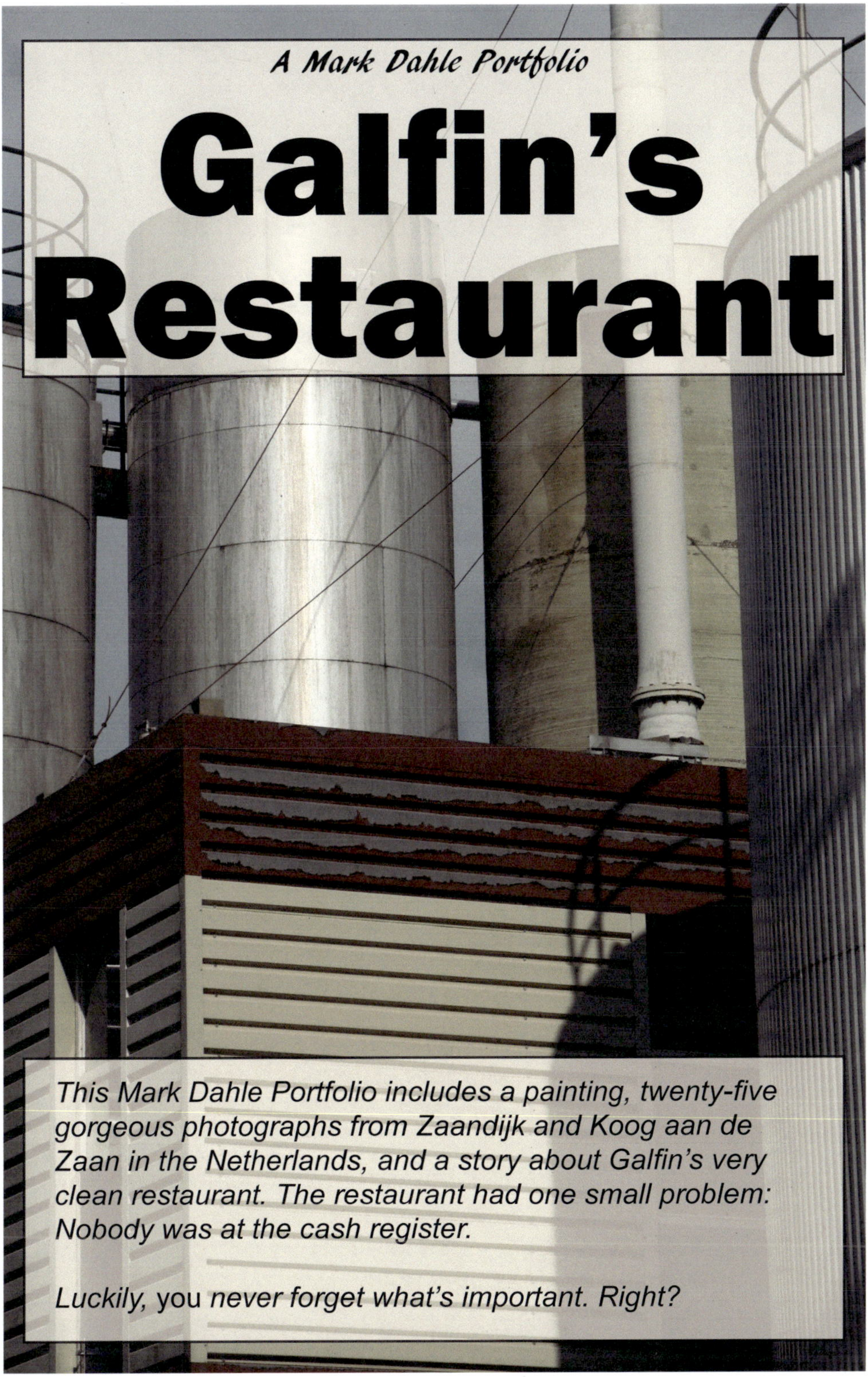

A Mark Dahle Portfolio

Galfin's Restaurant

This Mark Dahle Portfolio includes a painting, twenty-five gorgeous photographs from Zaandijk and Koog aan de Zaan in the Netherlands, and a story about Galfin's very clean restaurant. The restaurant had one small problem: Nobody was at the cash register.

Luckily, you never forget what's important. Right?

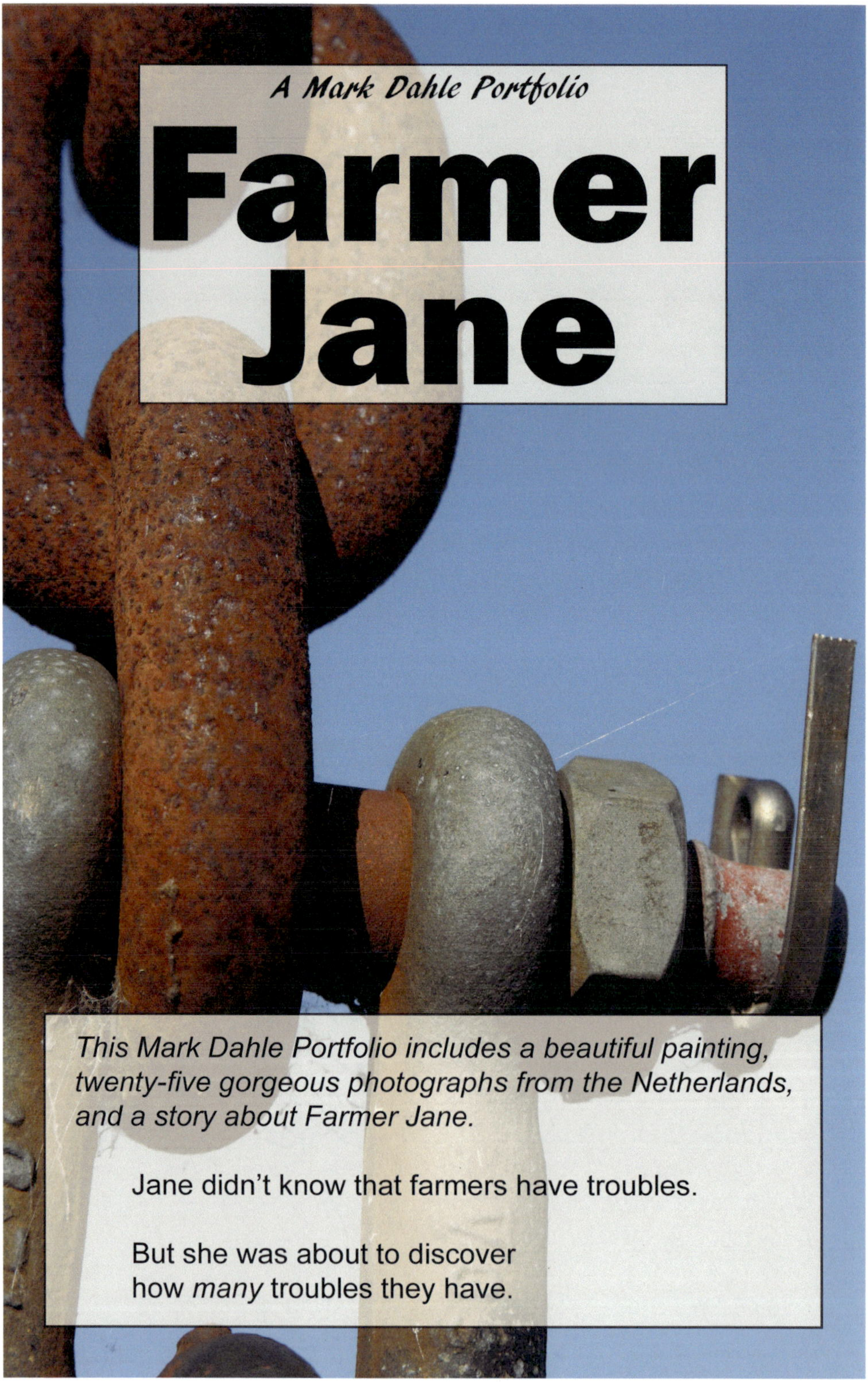

A Mark Dahle Portfolio

Farmer Jane

This Mark Dahle Portfolio includes a beautiful painting, twenty-five gorgeous photographs from the Netherlands, and a story about Farmer Jane.

Jane didn't know that farmers have troubles.

But she was about to discover
how *many* troubles they have.

Made in the USA
Columbia, SC
17 June 2025

59522617R00031